25 AWESOME FACTS ABOUT THE COAST GUARD

25 Awesome Facts About The Coast Guard:

Odd and Interesting Truths About America's Most-Forgotten Military Branch

By Brian Runion

The Claw of Knowledge

For information on reprinting portions of this book, contact Brian Runion at **clawofknowledge@gmail.com**.

Neither the United States Coast Guard nor any other component of the Department of Homeland Security or the Department of Defense has approved, endorsed, or authorized this book.

~

The views expressed herein are those of the author and are not to be construed as official or reflecting the views of the Commandant or of the U.S. Coast Guard.

To all the guardians of the coast, whether we remember them or not.

Thank You!

The following people are the reason this book exists. Because of their amazing contributions, you're reading these words right now!

The Following People Are Bona Fide Puddle Privateers:

Adam Petersen ▪ Autumn Carter ▪ Brad Clemons ▪ Colin & Emily Menendez ▪ CPO Rob Cox ▪ Jonathan Alier ▪ Krystal Marx ▪ Matthew Pollio ▪ Michael Allen ▪ Michael Hudec ▪ Miranda Brudzinski ▪ Nicole Roberts ▪ Noah & Eli Spencer, Grandsons of Commander P.W. Spencer ▪ OS1 Jim Bayer ▪ Sandi Fox ▪ Scott Thomas ▪ Sheila Hattarki Reynolds ▪ Stacey & Clay Rogers ▪ Stacey Campbell - CG Mom ▪ The Ingram Family ▪ The Paggi Family ▪ The Smiths ▪ The Stevick Family ▪ Theresa Roldan ▪ Todd Krinke

The Following People Are Like Starfleet, Only Really Cynical About Everything:

Allen Hughey ▪ Bret M. Thomas ▪ Joe & Carly Koczarski ▪ Chrystin A. McLelland ▪ Clifford Grader ▪ Corinna Humphries ▪ Daniel Hockaday ▪ Daniel K. Pickles, CAPT, USCG ▪ David Young ▪ Edward Van Riper ▪ Fred Kuebler ▪ Greg Czerwonka ▪ Hannah Cronin ▪ Harold Gracey ▪ Heather Wilson ▪ Ian Starr ▪ Irene & Taylor ▪ Jamie Embry ▪ Jeffrey & Ana Oceguera ▪ Jennifer C. Wong ▪ Jerry Chapman ▪ Jim Herlong ▪ Joe Prado ▪ John Packard ▪ John Roddy ▪ Jon E. Fitzpatrick ▪ Joseph & Shannon Castañeda ▪ Karen Appel ▪ Kathleen Edwards ▪ Kelcie ▪ Kimberly Mourey ▪ Kyle Ensley ▪ Lauren Carter ▪ LCDR Brandy Parker ▪ Lisa ▪ Lloyd Gorman, CWO4, USCG (Ret.) ▪ Louise Carter ▪ Marty Burnham, ETC (Ret.) ▪ Matt Baker ▪ Matt Duncan ▪ Matt Malacaria ▪ Matt Panciocco ▪ Maureen Johnson ▪ Michael Kavanagh ▪ Mike Jarbeau ▪ Mr. & Mrs. Corey A. Meeks ▪ Nathaniel J. ▪ Robert Bied ▪ Rusty Dash, International Man of Mystery ▪ Sara Mooers ▪ Savanna F. ▪ Shadow Jones ▪ Shandra & Skye Edmond ▪ Steve ▪ The Cecchini Family ▪ The Cyr and Coyle Family ▪ The Raley's ▪ Tinunola Adelakin ▪ Tom Wieland ▪ Vince Taylor ▪ Zachary Frohn

The Following People Are Pretty Much Batman:

AJ Pulkkinen ▪ Amanda Morton ▪ Amy ▪ Bryan & Christina Thompson ▪ Bud & Linda Runion ▪ CDR William, Amber & Arwen Kintz ▪ CG Mom ▪ Chris Hepp ▪ Claire Kuffel ▪ Colleen Clark ▪ Craig S. Swirbliss, CAPT, USCG (Ret) ▪ Cuttermom ▪ David Tonon ▪ Debbie Kowalski ▪ E.W. ▪ Elisa ▪ Grayson Stalvey ▪ Holly Harrison ▪ James J. O'Brien ▪ Jiah "Kia" Barnett ▪ Kate Woods ▪ Ken Winterberger ▪ LCDR Wes Burns ▪ Lelea Seymour ▪ Maria Montoya ▪ ME1 Tom Gadomski ▪ Melissa Ownby ▪ Melissa St. John ▪ R & K Kramer ▪ Rebecca Templeton ▪ Ryan McElroy ▪ Sarah Lacey ▪ Say Jay Hynes ▪ Teresa Hunt ▪ The Everett Family ▪ The Pecoras ▪ The Saxon Family ▪ Tim Sommella ▪ Tina Schultz ▪ Yamil Hernandez

The Following People Rival the Exploits of The Esteemed Florence Finch:
Rebecca Tyson Smith and Damon Stuebner ▪ Jeff and DesaRae Janszen

The Following People Basically Drove A Landing Craft On D-Day (Or Would Have If They'd Been Alive At The Time)

These bios belong to people who went above and beyond to make sure this book got made! However, I did no research on them beforehand, so there's a decent chance the info here is made of lies.

Rachel & Chris Quatroche

Rachel Quatroche is a Coast Guard aviator and knows how to fly helicopters, planes, unicorns, dragons, Antarctica, fire, and probably the sun if she tried hard enough. She married her husband Chris on top of a mountain surrounded by meteorites and a lot of cool-looking mist. Chris grew a beard after leaving the Coast Guard, but may have shaved it by the time he reads this. Or maybe he grew a longer beard. I don't read minds. They currently live in the remote wilderness, far from civilization, and can only be reached by bear and/or jetpack.

Jennifer Runion

Jennifer Runion is my older sister and was my commanding officer long before either of us joined the Coast Guard. Thanks to her leadership growing up, I learned how to deal with authority at a young age, while she learned how to deal with unruly subordinates. When I asked her what she wanted for her stick-figure image, she said, "You know what I look like, right?" I do know what she looks like, and it's kind of like the stick-figure on the left.

IT3 Christopher J. Headley

Christopher "Jayhawk" Headley is a Coast Guard IT specialist who once rewired an entire Coast Guard Cutter to be the internet. No, not use the internet – to *be* the internet. Unfortunately, this also took up most of the Coast Guard's bandwidth and has led to server room flooding whenever anyone tries to Google "the ocean." As a result, the Coast Guard has set Material Condition Zebra on its internet browsers ever since. He is currently working on a fix, but it has a 50/50 shot of either ending civilization or curing cancer.

Peggy Ann West

Peggy Ann West is a myth that has been passed down through the ages. Her name was first discovered scrawled into the rock spires of Stonehenge, and also appears in an early draft of the Dead Sea Scrolls. Although her worshippers once held lavish banquets in her honor, they must now meet in secret, in forgotten caverns far below the city streets. On warm nights near the summer solstice, you can hear their distant chants as they call forth her spirit from the ether. Perhaps one day she will answer their cries and return.

A Coastie On Watch

If you're reading this book, you probably know A Coastie On Watch. A Coastie On Watch is the type of person who will always be there for you, rain or shine, night or day, even though A Coastie On Watch is probably kind of tired and hasn't gotten much sleep recently. A Coastie On Watch keeps busy, and is probably doing something very, very important right now. In fact, if you were just interrupted from reading this to respond to a search-and-rescue case, you might actually be A Coastie On Watch. Get back to work.

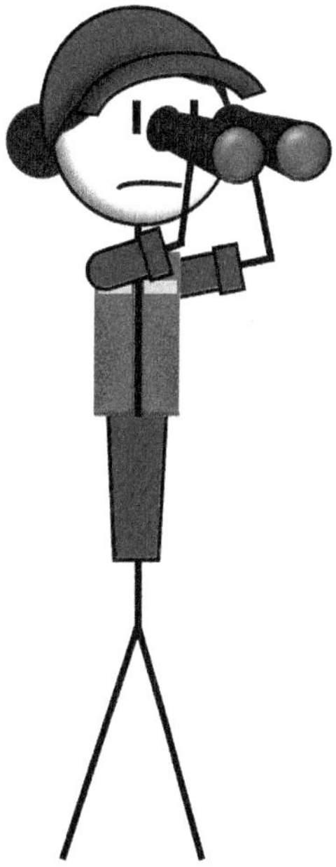

Foreword

This book wouldn't exist without the incredible support of a few thousand people online: people who read my work and shared it with others, who encouraged me to keep making comics and writing posts, and who wanted just as much as I did to see the Coast Guard's story told with all the beauty, hilarity, and cynicism it deserves. Without all those people, I would just be a guy sitting at a computer, quietly laughing at his own comics. Instead, I'm a guy writing a book, and that's a much better thing to be.

I started The Claw of Knowledge in early 2014. Back then, I wasn't planning to draw comics or even to specifically talk about the Coast Guard; I was just looking for something I could do while waiting to hear back on job applications.

It wasn't an easy time for me. I had left the Coast Guard two years earlier to go to grad school, planning to work as a foreign policy analyst once I got out. Unfortunately, by the time I finished school, the funding for the work I wanted to do had dried up. The Coast Guard was on a hiring freeze, and my narrow window to rejoin the service had closed. Still, as a veteran Coast Guard officer, my prospects weren't terrible by any means, and within a few months, I was on the verge of starting my dream job: a once-in-a-lifetime opportunity to work at Stanford University, managing a working group on foreign policy.

Now, that may sound boring to most of you, but for me, it was like getting pulled out of touch football to play for the NFL. The working group I'd be managing contained two former Secretaries of State, as well as a gamut of the very International Relations rockstars I'd studied as a cadet. My job would be to guide their discussions, to choose what literature they'd be reading, and to sit in a room as they spoke and bask in their collective brilliance.

I was all set to move to Palo Alto when the worst happened: the government shut down, and Stanford lost a bunch of funding. I got a call from the professor in charge of my program, and she said that as much as she wanted to bring me on, the University had decided it would be cheaper to transfer the job to a PhD student.

It just about killed me.

To make matters worse, the shutdown also took away the funding for my back-up jobs. Everything I was under consideration for was put on hold, and I spent months in limbo, not knowing when – or if – any of those jobs would materialize. I resigned myself to freelance work as a way to survive, and created The Claw of Knowledge to keep myself sane. While it proved a welcome distraction, the site barely registered a gurgle at first, bringing in a few readers here and there – mostly friends and family – to look at my strange, grimacing stick figures.

Then suddenly, on Memorial Day, traffic shot up. From a handful of visits every day, I suddenly had thousands. Almost all of them were to look at one post I had written three months earlier:

Five Awesome Facts About The Coast Guard.

Over the next few weeks, I got a flood of messages and comments from readers. People told me how they'd hung the drawings up at work, or how they'd used the post to explain the Coast Guard to their friends and family. They asked if they could make t-shirts or posters, and if it was okay to share it with their friends on Facebook. That's when I realized that – beyond just writing a funny blog post – I'd touched on something that didn't really exist for the Coast Guard: an entertaining, easy-to-understand primer on just what our service *does*.

That's what this book is meant to be: a celebration of the little-known quirks and accomplishments that make the Coast Guard such an unusual, wonderful, and terrible organization to work for. All the things that make it both indispensable and ignored. All the things that make me proud to be a Coastie.

I hope you enjoy reading it as much as I enjoyed making it.

-Brian

A Brief Note on Accuracy

This book is meant to be a mixture of humor and history – but mostly humor. While everything in here is based on actual research and can be backed up with sources, my goal wasn't to write an academic tome: it was to make something fun and engaging that celebrates the long legacy of the Coast Guard. While I don't deliberately deviate from history, the format of this book forces me to simplify. That means that no matter how hard I try, some of the nuance gets lost in writing. I'd encourage everyone who wants to learn more about these and other Coast Guard stories to check out the sources I've listed in the back of the book, as well as the official Coast Guard Historian's site at uscg.mil/history. Most of my best information came from there.

That being said, I did make some artistic choices that I know aren't accurate, for the sake of maintaining the book's feel. This includes sometimes using the term "Coast Guard" when I really mean "Revenue-Marine," "Life-Saving Service," or "Revenue Cutter Service," as well as being a bit imprecise with uniforms. Throughout the book, I mostly choose to portray Coasties wearing modernized Coast Guard attire rather than something appropriate to their eras or situations. The reason for this is because, prior to ~~stealing the Air Force's~~ designing its own uniform in the 1970s, the Coast Guard dressed almost identically to the U.S. Navy. Since I want all of the Coasties in this book to be instantly recognizable as such, I've decided depict them wearing whatever uniform I felt would ensure they won't be mistaken for another service.

So in other words, I've tried to solve the problem we have in real life.

Go Coast Guard.

I USED TO BE IN THE COAST GUARD...

And I'd always get a lot of questions whenever I walked around in uniform. Questions like "How long have you been in the Air Force?" and "What time does my train leave?" These were all important questions, of course, but I rarely had the answers.

CAN YOU DELIVER THIS FOR ME?

Sometimes, though, people would realize I was in the Coast Guard, and they'd ask me questions about that. Most of them were pretty basic – "Is the Coast Guard like the National Guard?" "Is it really a part of the military?" Others were more complex:

"Do you deploy overseas?"

"Do you really just stand there and guard the coast all day?

Warning:
Coast!
Much like how the Air Force is literally just a force of air...

To answer some of these questions, I decided to make up a list.

25 AWESOME FACTS ABOUT THE COAST GUARD

#1 WE'RE NOT JUST LIFEGUARDS (OR COAST-GUARDS)

The Coast Guard is the world's foremost search-and-rescue organization, but that's not all. We operate all over the world, in every ocean, on every continent. We fight pirates and drug runners, clean up oil spills, enforce laws and treaties, and explore the ice shelves at both poles. Our missions routinely take us into conditions that make other mariners turn back: into ice, into storms, into sinking ships. We boldly go where no other service wants to go.

We're like Starfleet, if Starfleet was really cynical about everything.

LIEUTENANT RUNION, PREPARE TO BEAM ABOARD THE ALIEN SHIP. BUT DO NOT VIOLATE THE PRIME DIRECTIVE!
I'M REALLY MORE OF A *STAR WARS* GUY, SIR.

#2 THE COAST GUARD ONLY HAS ABOUT 46,000 PEOPLE, BUT PROTECTS OVER 4.7 MILLION SQUARE MILES OF OCEAN

That's over 100 square miles per person.

Warning:
Ocean!

"Still beats the Academy."

We do more than just float around, of course. We have ships and aircraft stationed everywhere from Guam to Puerto Rico, from Alaska to American Samoa. We take part in multinational military exercises, train foreign coast guards, and even protect oil platforms in the Middle East. And we do it all with outdated equipment, dwindling manpower, and less money every year than the other services spend in a week.

#3 FOR SEVEN YEARS, THE COAST GUARD WAS OUR ONLY NAVY

The Coast Guard started life as the Revenue-Marine. It was founded by Alexander Hamilton in 1790 to stop the smugglers and pirates who were sapping the U.S. of its trade revenue. Without the Revenue-Marine, the United States likely would've gone bankrupt before it even had its second president. Not only that, but from 1790 until the launch of the first ships of the U.S. Navy in 1797, the Coast Guard's forerunner service was the only naval defense force the U.S. had.

That makes the Coast Guard the nation's oldest continuous sea-going service, although the Navy likes to point out that the Continental Navy - their predecessor - existed from 1775 to 1783. Since there was a 15-year gap where no Navy existed, which one of us 'came first' remains a hotly-debated issue.

WATCH IT, NOOBS!
U.S. COAST GUARD

#4 THE COAST GUARD DROVE THE LANDING CRAFT ON D-DAY

And in every major amphibious assault during World War II. The Coast Guard's experience piloting small boats in rough surf made them exceptionally qualified to take troops and equipment ashore. The landing craft themselves offered little protection, though, leaving their crews vulnerable to sniper fire, machine guns, and mortars. Landing routes were poorly charted and often mined. It fell to the ingenuity of each coxswain to deliver his troops safely to the beach.

All in all, the Coast Guard manned roughly a hundred vessels on D-Day, ranging from landing craft to the operation's flagship, the *USS BAYFIELD*. Not only did these craft put thousands of troops ashore, they also saved the lives of more than 400 soldiers and sailors stranded on the waves.

THIS IS WHY WE INVENTED MATTER TRANSPORTERS!

#5 A COAST GUARD OFFICER ONCE BLUFFED 300 GERMANS INTO SURRENDERING A FORT

Following the Allied invasion of Normandy in 1944, the German Army still held most of the critical port of Cherbourg, France. This included pockets of resistance throughout the city, a network of mines and boobytraps, and the stronghold of Fort du Homet, where 300 Germans held 50 American paratroopers prisoner. Lieutenant Commander Quentin Walsh, a Coast Guard logistics officer and military planner, realized that unless the Germans were pushed out of Cherbourg, the Allies would be unable to bring in supplies to fuel the war effort.

Walsh led his team of troops and fought from house to house, capturing 400 enemy soldiers in the process. Even so, Walsh knew that unless Fort du Homet fell, the Germans would continue to shell the port. They couldn't simply blow it up – there were U.S. prisoners inside. So he pulled out a white scarf and walked up to the gates, where he told the Germans he had come to negotiate their surrender. With only 16 men accompanying him, Walsh convinced the Germans that he had them surrounded and that there was no escape. The Germans turned over their weapons, freed the American paratroopers, and gave up control of the fort.

For his actions, Walsh received the Navy Cross.

WE'RE JUST HERE TO DELIVER YOUR MAIL!

Important Events in the

CIRCA 200,000 B.C.: EARLY HUMANS FIRST ENCOUNTER WATER, PRESUMABLY TRY TO AVOID DROWNING.

CIRCA 45,000 B.C.: PACIFIC ISLANDERS INEXPLICABLY REACH THE PACIFIC ISLES.

MAYBE WE SWAM.

476 A.D.: ROME FALLS AND THE DARK AGES BEGIN. WITHOUT THE ROMAN NAVY PATROLLING THE SEAS, MARITIME TRADE VANISHES FROM WESTERN EUROPE.

UH...I MEANT TO DO THAT.

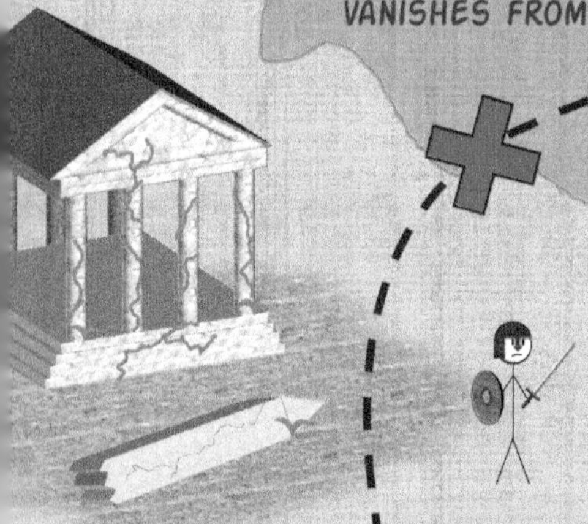

CIRCA 45 A.D.: ROMAN EMPEROR CLAUDIUS SINKS A GIANT TRANSPORT BARGE BY FILLING IT WITH CONCRETE. HE THEN USES IT AS THE FOUNDATION FOR AN OFFSHORE LIGHTHOUSE.

History of Coast-Guarding

CIRCA 3000 B.C.: EGYPTIANS CONSTRUCT THE FIRST PLANK-HULLED SHIPS, ALLOWING PEOPLE TO SINK FURTHER FROM LAND THAN EVER BEFORE.

CIRCA 600 B.C.: HANNO THE NAVIGATOR SAILS FROM CARTHAGE TO WEST AFRICA, RESULTING IN ONE OF THE EARLIEST-KNOWN SETS OF SAILING DIRECTIONS AND A WARNING NOT TO MESS WITH GORILLAS.

490 B.C.: PERSIAN TROOPS LAND AT MARATHON. IT REMAINS THE LARGEST AMPHIBIOUS ASSAULT UNTIL WORLD WAR II AND MAKES PEOPLE WANT TO RUN LONG DISTANCES.

I'M MORE OF A SPRINTER.

CIRCA 150 B.C.: THE *ARTHASHASTRA*, AN ANCIENT INDIAN TREATISE ON STATECRAFT, PROPOSES A CHIEF OF SHIPPING TO OVERSEE MARITIME RESCUE, CUSTOMS COLLECTION, AND THE SECURITY OF FERRY SYSTEMS. THE SAME TEXT RECOMMENDS CUTTING OFF THE THUMBS OF WEAVERS WHO PERFORM POORLY.

280 B.C.: THE GREEKS BUILD THE FIRST FULL-FLEDGED LIGHTHOUSE AT ALEXANDRIA. IT'S KEPT LIT WITH CARTLOADS OF WOOD HAULED TO THE TOP BY MULES.

HOW DO YOU TURN IT OFF?

OFFICIAL MISSIONS OF THE U.S. COAST GUARD

- MARITIME LAW ENFORCEMENT
- PORTS, WATERWAYS, AND COASTAL SECURITY
- DRUG INTERDICTION
- AIDS TO NAVIGATION
- SEARCH AND RESCUE
- LIVING MARINE RESOURCES
- MARINE SAFETY
- DEFENSE READINESS
- MIGRANT INTERDICTION
- MARINE ENVIRONMENTAL PROTECTION
- ICE OPERATIONS

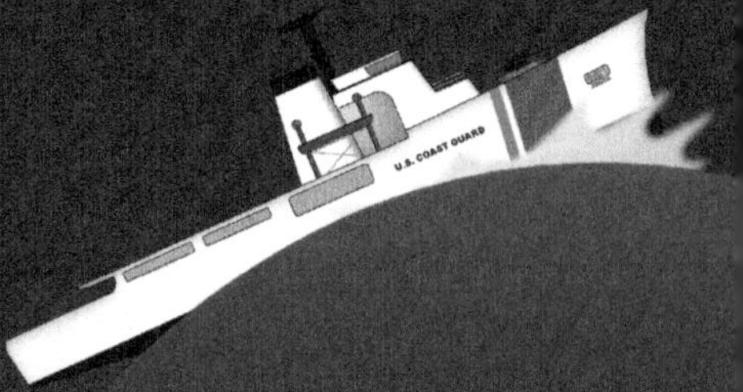

ACTUAL MISSIONS OF THE U.S. COAST GUARD

- SAILING OVER WAVES BIGGER THAN OUR BOATS
- BEING CONFUSED FOR AIRLINE PILOTS
- DOING THINGS THE NAVY TAKES CREDIT FOR
- CHASING DOWN FIREWORKS PEOPLE MISTOOK FOR DISTRESS FLARES
- GLUING 50-YEAR-OLD BOATS BACK TOGETHER
- DEVELOPING AN IMMUNITY TO CAFFEINE
- SAVING PEOPLE WHO TRIED TO CROSS THE OCEAN USING GOOGLE MAPS
- DISPOSING OF ILLICIT DRUGS WORTH MORE THAN OUR ENTIRE BUDGET
- FENDING OFF PENGUIN ATTACKS

HALT!
Warning:
Coast!

FROM AZTEC SHORE TO LOW EARTH ORBIT:

FIVE PLACES YOU'LL FIND THE COAST GUARD

#6 THERE ARE COAST GUARD ASTRONAUTS

When you think about it, being in orbit is kind of like being off the coast: you can see land, but you can't get back to it without ~~getting eaten by sharks~~ exploding in a vacuum. Er...Okay, so it's not a perfect analogy. But the Coast Guard has nevertheless fielded two NASA astronauts, who crewed the Space Shuttle and International Space Station. They credit their success in space to their unique experiences in the Coast Guard: working with small crews in tight quarters, solving problems using limited resources, and learning to fight off large, tentacled monsters that threaten to destroy your vessel.

DON'T WORRY, I'VE GOT THIS.

#7 THE COAST GUARD FOUGHT IN AFGHANISTAN

And in every American war since 1790.

Now, if you think the Coast Guard can't do much in a landlocked country, then you're not thinking like a Coastie. Shore or no shore, the service has over 200 years' experience hunting rogue groups like pirates and drug cartels: a skillset that also makes them good at fighting terror networks. Alongside Coalition forces in Afghanistan, the Coast Guard helped disrupt insurgent groups and protect the lives of Afghan citizens leading up to the national elections.

In fact, thanks to the Coast Guard's unconventional methods, they were even able to give the other services a few pointers.

...AND YOU JUST WANT ME TO STAND HERE?
DON'T YOU KNOW *ANYTHING* ABOUT GUARDING?!
Warning: Land!

#8 THE NAVY ONCE USED US IN *THEIR* RECRUITING POSTER

The aftermath of Hurricane Katrina. A Navy helicopter crewman stares wistfully out across the flooded streets of New Orleans, knowing he's done his part to save lives. At the bottom of the poster, a caption urges you to join the Navy, where you can "provide aid to the victims of natural disasters" and "fight sea piracy." Sounds pretty cool, huh?

EVER WANTED TO GUARD THINGS NEAR A COAST?
ONLY ONE SERVICE DOES THAT
NAVY
WE'RE WICKED AWESOME

Artist's Conception

Except it's not a Navy helicopter crewman, or even a Navy helicopter. It's a picture of a Coast Guard petty officer, riding in a Coast Guard helicopter, doing Coast Guard things, plastered into an ad for how you can join the Navy and do a whole bunch of things the Coast Guard does.

Now, I don't want to fault the Navy too much. They play a huge role in disaster relief efforts, like the tsunamis in Japan and Southeast Asia, or the 2010 earthquake in Haiti. But seriously, Navy…you have aircraft carriers, jet fighters, and submarines, yet you decided to skip all of those things and use a picture of one of our guys, in one of our helicopters, to represent *your* service?

Thanks. We love that you realize how cool we are.

JOIN THE
COAST GUARD
IN MOCKING THE NAVY FOR
SECRETLY BEING JEALOUS OF US

#9 THE COAST GUARD HERDED 400 REINDEER TO THE ARCTIC

In November 1897, eight whaling ships got trapped in the ice north of Point Barrow, Alaska. The 275 sailors saw little hope for survival: even if the ice didn't crush them, they'd starve to death before long.

Revenue Cutter *BEAR* sailed north to mount a rescue. Because the Bering Sea had already frozen, the cutter's only hope of getting food to the whalers was to send a small team overland. Three volunteers, led by Lieutenant David Jarvis, set out from the edge of the ice with sleds and dogs. Since they couldn't haul enough supplies by themselves to feed the whalers, Jarvis used his fluency in Inuit to barter for reindeer. They gathered around 400 of the creatures and herded them across 1,500 miles of frozen tundra.

The journey took three months of hard travel, in the permanent dark of Arctic winter. Jarvis and his team nearly died many times: stuck in blizzards, lost in the wilderness, or freezing in -45° weather. And when they reached the ships, their job wasn't done. The whalers were sickly and had fallen into disarray. Jarvis imposed order, fed them, and built shelters from the wrecked ships. They kept the whalers alive until July, when *BEAR* broke through the ice and rescued them. It was September before they returned to Seattle.

I can only imagine what their travel claims looked like.

SORRY...THIS FORM DOESN'T HAVE A CODE FOR "DOGSLED."
...YOU SAVED YOUR RECEIPTS, RIGHT?

#10 THE COAST GUARD IS THE ONLY MILITARY FORCE ALLOWED TO PATROL THE GREAT LAKES

And the reason for that dates back over 200 years. During the War of 1812, the British Navy suffered a major defeat on Lake Erie. Wanting to avoid a second one, after the War they signed a treaty with the U.S. that limited both sides to one small patrol boat each per Lake. Under the modern interpretation, still honored by Canada, it means the Navy isn't allowed to sail the Lakes for anything other than training.

As a result, only the Coast Guard can patrol those waters, and it's a big job: at 4,500 miles, the U.S. has a bigger coastline on the Great Lakes than it does on the East or West Coasts. Every year, the Coast Guard saves hundreds of lives in the region and also breaks winter ice to keep ships moving. Prior to 2006, Coast Guard cutters patrolled the Lakes unarmed, but due to rising security concerns, the service began arming its Great Lakes vessels with light machine guns.

Because you never know when Canada will strike.

Important Events In The

WHAT? I HATE PAPERWORK.

789: NORSE RAIDERS EXPLOIT NORTHERN EUROPE'S LACK OF ORGANIZED FLEETS TO INVADE THE BRITISH ISLES. THE FIRST PERSON THEY KILL IS THE CUSTOMS OFFICER.

CIRCA 1100: SETTLERS ALONG THE NORTH COAST OF RUSSIA BUILD THE FIRST ICE-BREAKING SAILING SHIPS. WHY THEY DON'T USE THEM TO SETTLE SOMEWHERE WARMER IS UNCLEAR.

Ye Toll
HEY! GET BACK HERE!

1157: MERCHANT SAILING RETURNS TO NORTHERN EUROPE, LARGELY AS A WAY TO SKIRT LAND TOLLS.

1274: A MONGOL FLEET INVADES JAPAN, BUT IS DESTROYED IN A TYPHOON. A SECOND FLEET ARRIVES 7 YEARS LATER, ONLY TO BE DESTROYED THE SAME WAY.

...THIRD TIME'S A CHARM, RIGHT?

History of Coast-Guarding

1296: The first-recorded use of buoys as a guide to mariners is noted in an Italian sailing text.

1450: Venice peaks as a maritime trading power, with over 3000 merchant galleys. Venice's shipyard employs 16,000 laborers and can build an entire ship in a single day.

WATCH IT! SHE'S NEW!

1381: Portugal becomes the first nation to use cannons as a coastal defense. But that doesn't stop them from being attacked by land.

Circa 1400: The Mayan port city of Tulum places lit torches atop its temple towers. By aligning the beacons, local ships can find the safe channel through the reef into the harbor.

DIAGRAM OF A COASTIE

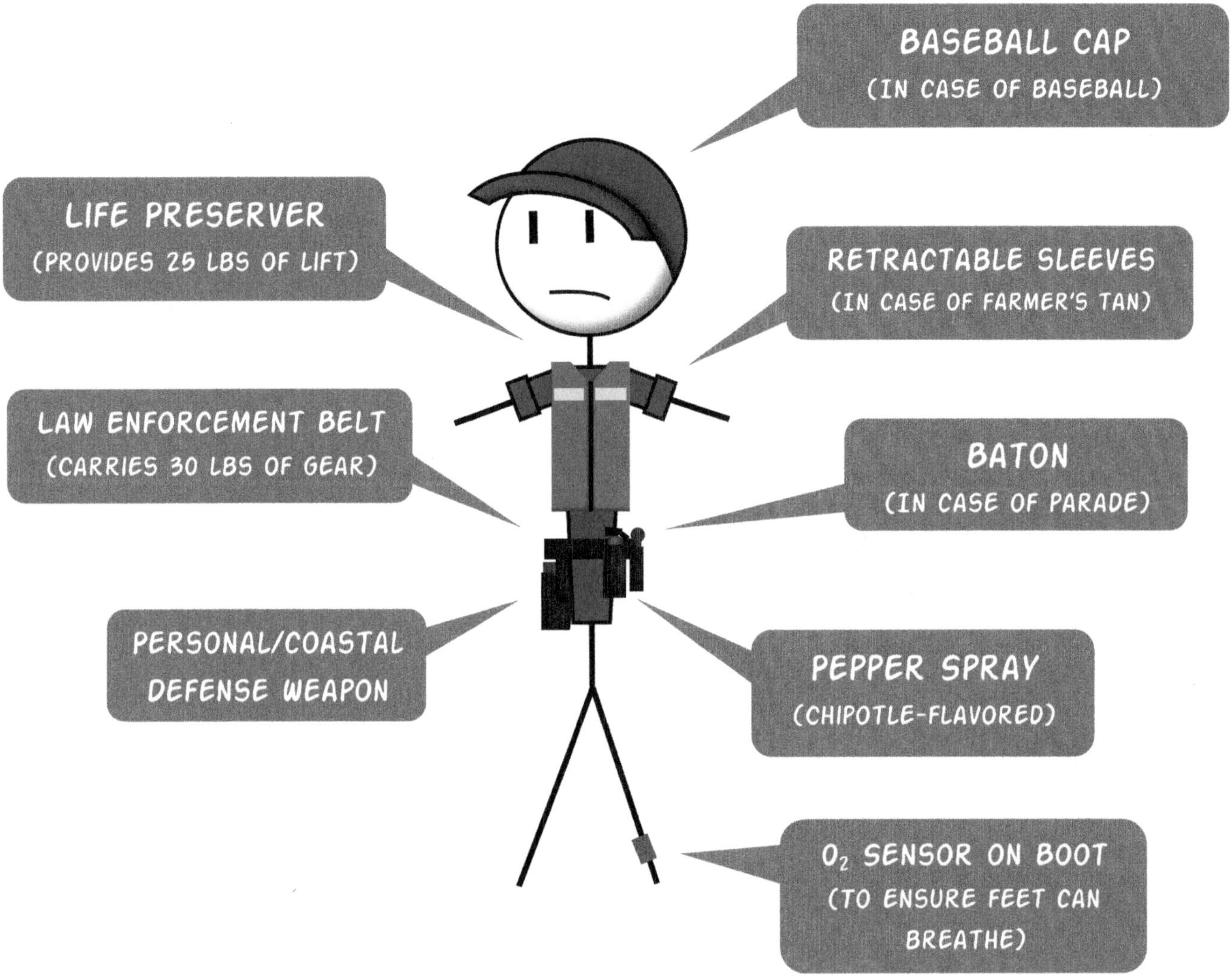

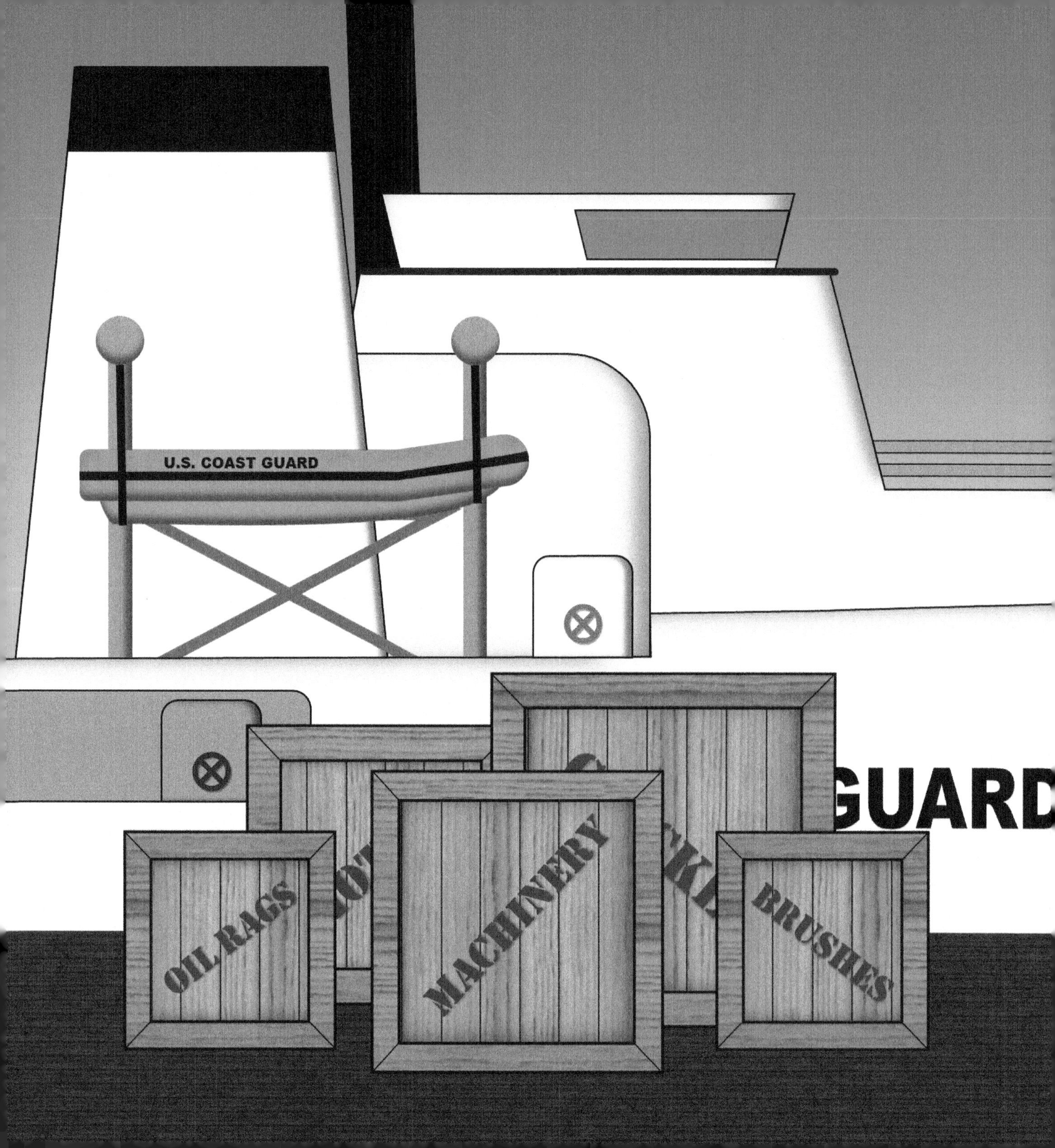
U.S. COAST GUARD
GUARD
OIL RAGS
MACHINERY
BRUSHES

Our Only Armor Is Hull Paint:

Five Ways The Coast Guard Scrapes By

#11 "YOU HAVE TO GO OUT, BUT YOU DON'T HAVE TO COME BACK" WASN'T EXACTLY A JOKE

If you've spent enough time around Coasties, you've probably heard the phrase, "You have to go out, but you don't have to come back." It sounds like something we say to amuse ourselves: a bit of gallows humor by people used to risking their lives on a daily basis. It's not.

The phrase comes from a particularly dangerous rescue off Cape Hatteras in the early 1900s: a young surfman warned his captain, Patrick Etheridge, that even if they made it out to the sinking ship through the rough surf, they'd almost certainly never make it back to shore. Etheridge replied, "The Blue Book says we've got to go out and it doesn't say a damn thing about having to come back." So they went.

But you see, Etheridge wasn't kidding. According to the "Blue Book" – the regulations for the service – surfmen weren't allowed to abort a rescue simply because they deemed it impossible: they actually had to *prove* it was impossible by rowing out into the surf and trying. And if they failed, they had to try again another way. And again. And again. Until they either died or ran out of rescue gear.

Because that's what Coasties do.

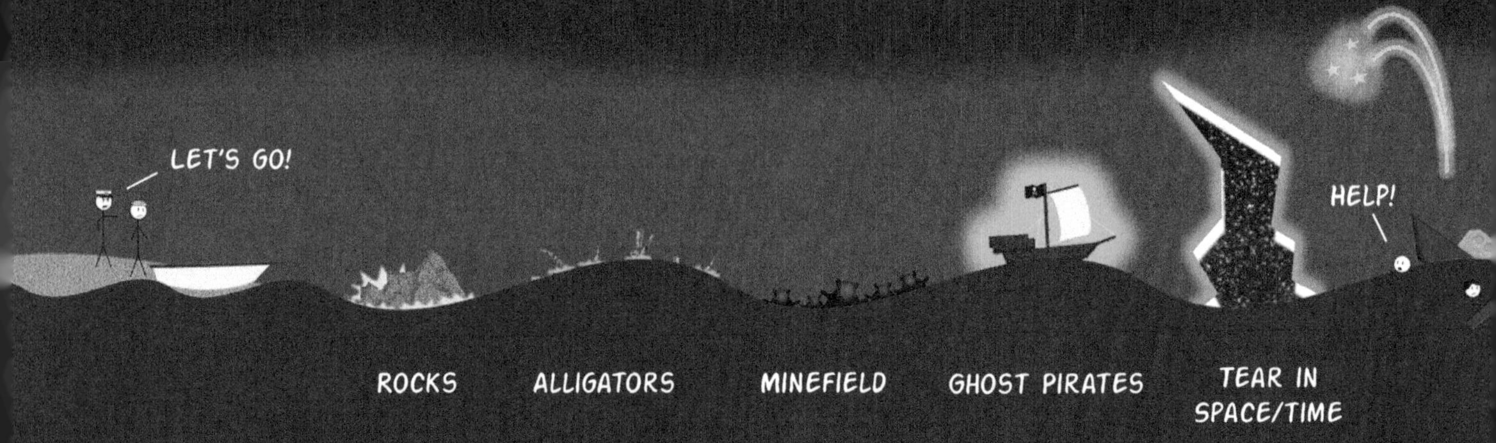

#12 THE COAST GUARD TRAINED RESCUE PIGEONS

The Coast Guard is endlessly innovative, mostly because it has to be. In 1979, it launched Project Sea Hunt: a program to train pigeons as rescue spotters.

It wasn't without its troubles.

Pigeons are better than humans at picking out shapes and colors at sea. They would ride in Plexiglas bubbles beneath Coast Guard helicopters, and whenever they'd spot something in international orange (the color of distress gear), they'd peck a switch and alert the crew. Although it may sound ridiculous, the birds were actually quite effective: during trial runs, they spotted target objects almost three times as often as humans, and almost always faster.

Sadly, budget cuts forced the program to close in 1983, before it even…er…got off the ground.

#13 THE COAST GUARD FLEW B-17s

When World War II ended in 1945, the Army still had B-17 Flying Fortresses rolling off the assembly lines. The Coast Guard, being ever-resourceful, realized that these bombers' 2,000-mile range and sturdy construction made them ideal search-and-rescue craft. Even better, the Army had already designed a 12-person lifeboat that could be slung under the plane and dropped to survivors via parachute. The Coast Guard quickly worked to acquire 18 of the aircraft.

VICTORY!
SO...UH...YOU STILL USING THIS?
WAR OVER!

From 1946 until 1959, B-17s served the Coast Guard under the naval designation "PB-1G," mapping coastlines, tracking icebergs, and aiding survivors at sea. The planes flew in the harsh conditions of Alaska and Greenland, as well as the East and West Coasts, until they were replaced by the long-lived C-130.

#14 THE MAN WHO DESIGNED THE COKE BOTTLE ALSO DESIGNED THE COAST GUARD STRIPE

In the 1960s, the Coast Guard had a bit of a problem: hardly anyone knew the service existed. Even the people we saved thought they'd been pulled out of the water by the Navy, not the Coast Guard. Raymond Loewy, the industrial designer behind stylish items like the Studebaker Commodore and the now-iconic Coca-Cola bottle, proposed a solution. He had just redrawn the paint scheme for Air Force One, giving him some clout with President Kennedy. He suggested that the Coast Guard develop a brand identity: the plain white cutters bore nothing to set them apart from Navy ships.

So Loewy drew up a set of parallel stripes of red and blue, set at a 64-degree angle. The stripes were first tested out on a handful of units – cutters, buildings, aircraft, vehicles – but by the 1970s, were on practically everything the service owned (including, unwisely, the ties on women's dress uniforms). While some were skeptical at first, the look became so closely associated with coast-guarding that virtually every nation's sea-going rescue service now uses some version of Loewy's stripe.

Which, of course, is why we no longer get mistaken for anything else.

#15 THE COAST GUARD WAS NEARLY ABOLISHED

When Congress authorized the Coast Guard in 1914, they designed the legislation so that the service could be brought under control of the Navy in times of war. Just three short years later, this rule was tested out: the Coast Guard, its personnel, and its ships became property of the Navy to fight World War I.

But as the war wound down, the Navy grew reluctant to give the Coast Guard back. The Secretary of the Navy, as well as his Assistant Secretary – a dastardly man named Franklin Roosevelt – wanted the Coast Guard to remain permanently in Navy hands. But that's not the worst part: so did 90% of Coast Guard officers. See, they had all received temporary promotions during the war, and leaving the Navy meant being demoted back. The Coast Guard's enlisted, on the other hand, would be demoted if they *stayed* with the Navy, as the Navy didn't view the Coast Guard's humanitarian skillset – boarding ships, saving lives, and piloting boats in rough surf – as having a place in their organization.

Only about 25 of the Coast Guard's 240 officers fought to keep the fledgling service alive. Thankfully, one of these men was the Coast Guard's Commandant (and guy on the left in Fact 9), Commodore Ellsworth Bertholf. Bertholf argued that the Navy and the Coast Guard, although similar, served opposite purposes, and that if the Coast Guard were to disappear into the Navy, its unique skillset would be lost forever.

Bertholf's testimony helped stop a Congressional bill that would have merged the two services permanently, although the fight to keep the Coast Guard alive hadn't ended. Over the next few years, proponents of the merger – even high-ranking members of the Coast Guard – tried and failed to garner support from Congress or the President to fuse the services into one monolithic, grey-hulled force.

We're all lucky they failed. In critical moments throughout the last century – in World War II, in Vietnam, in in Hurricane Katrina – the skills the Navy dismissed as unnecessary in 1918 have not only proven indispensable, they're ones the Coast Guard has taught to the Navy in times of need.

As we in the service like to say, we are the hard nucleus around which the Navy forms. In war and peace.

MOTRIN

~~A System of Revenue Cutters~~

~~THE REVENUE-MARINE~~

~~THE REVENUE CUTTER SERVICE~~

~~NINJA AWESOME FLEET~~

U.S. COAST GUARD

~~DEPARTMENT OF THE TREASURY~~

~~Department of the Navy~~

~~COAST JUSTICE LEAGUE~~

~~Department of Transportation~~

DEPARTMENT OF HOMELAND SECURITY

Important Events In The

1656: THE DUTCH TREASURE SHIP *VERGULDE DRAECK* SINKS OFF OF WESTERN AUSTRALIA, LEADING TO A 3-YEAR, MULTI-SHIP SEARCH-AND-RESCUE MISSION. THE CREW SURVIVES THE WRECK, BUT IS NEVER FOUND.

UH...WE WERE NEVER HERE.

1691: THE OWNER OF A LONDON COFFEE HOUSE STARTS COMPILING AND PRINTING INFO HE GATHERS FROM SHIPPING MERCHANTS WHO VISIT HIS SHOP. THIS PUBLICATION BECOMES KNOWN AS LLOYD'S LIST.

MISSED ME!

1716: BOSTON LIGHT IS THE FIRST LIGHTHOUSE CONSTRUCTED IN NORTH AMERICA. IT IS DESTROYED 60 YEARS LATER BY GEORGE WASHINGTON TO KEEP IT OUT OF BRITISH HANDS.

1702: NATIONS BEGIN TO ADOPT THE 'CANNON SHOT' RULE: THE NOTION THAT COASTAL TERRITORY EXTENDS AS FAR AS A CANNONBALL FLIES (I.E., 3 MILES). THIS RULE PERSISTS UNTIL THE 20TH CENTURY.

KIA!

History of Coast-Guarding

1520: THE AGE OF PIRACY BEGINS IN THE CARIBBEAN. PIRATE SHIPS ARE SURPRISINGLY WELL-ORGANIZED, AND SAILORS OFTEN HAVE THE RIGHT TO VOTE ON SHIPS' RULES.
SO...NOT LIKE COAST GUARD CUTTERS.
1502: THE FIRST-RECORDED CARIBBEAN HURRICANE HITS HISPANIOLA. IT SINKS 21 SHIPS AND KILLS 500 SAILORS.
1737: THE FIRST MODERN MARITIME LIFE-SAVING STATION IS ORGANIZED IN CHINA. IT TAKES THE WEST ANOTHER 50 YEARS TO CATCH ON.
GUESS I'LL JUST KEEP TREADING, THEN.
1755: A MASSIVE EARTHQUAKE DESTROYS LISBON. RESIDENTS FLEE TO THE SHORE FOR SAFETY, ONLY TO BE DROWNED BY A TSUNAMI.
Warning: Coast!
No... Really

73

It Pays To Be A Puddle Pirate:

Five Times Shallow-Water Sailing Saved The Day

#16 THE COAST GUARD HOLDS THE RECORD FOR LONGEST OVERSEAS DEPLOYMENT

At the start of the Cold War in 1952, the Coast Guard teamed up with the State Department to launch Coast Guard Cutter *COURIER*, a converted military cargo vessel housing the largest broadcast antenna ever placed on a ship. *COURIER* spent 12 years operating in the waters around the Greek island of Rhodes – the longest any U.S. military ship has gone without returning to an American port. By operating so close to shore, *COURIER* avoided international prohibitions against at-sea broadcasting. She aired news reports, jazz music, and cultural programming for the citizens of the Soviet Bloc, helping to pierce the Iron Curtain and provide an alternative to Soviet propaganda.

COURIER so frustrated the USSR's leaders that they actually threatened to send submarines to sink her. None ever did - but maybe they just had a soft spot for jazz.

#17 THE MARINES GOT TO MONTEZUMA'S HALLS BY LANDING ON THE AZTEC SHORE

If there's one military marching song that everyone knows, it's definitely not *Semper Paratus*. Rather, it's the Marine Corps hymn, with its famous opener: "From the Halls of Montezuma, to the Shores of Tripoli." (You're singing it in your head now, admit it.)

That line, of course, refers to two defining conflicts from the Marine Corps' first century of existence: the Barbary War, against the pirates of North Africa, and the Mexican War of 1846, in which the Marines captured Chapultepec Castle in Mexico City, formerly the stronghold of Aztec king Montezuma.

But did you ever wonder how the Marines *got* to Mexico? I'll give you a hint: the first line of *Semper Paratus* is "From Aztec Shore to Arctic Zone." That's right: ~~the Coast Guard left them in the Arctic~~ the Revenue Cutter Service dropped off the Marines and Army in Veracruz, Mexico to start their six-month push inland. Working alongside the Navy, the RCS used its shallow-water steamboats to ferry troops ashore, blockade the port, and shell Mexican positions. The Aztec shore led to Montezuma's halls.

Now, it's true that since Mexico didn't have much of a Navy, the Revenue Cutter Service only played a small part in the war. But what makes the Battle of Veracruz special is that it brought the Army, Navy, Marines, and Coast Guard together for the first major amphibious assault in American history – 97 years before they'd team up to do the same thing in World War II.

USM
USM
USM
THIS WAS FUN, GUYS! LET'S DO THIS EVERY CENTURY!

#18 THE COAST GUARD ENFORCED THE OIL EMBARGO ON IRAQ

When the U.N. placed an embargo on Iraq following the Persian Gulf War, the Iraqi government started sending smuggling ships to run oil to Iran, since they could no longer sell it on the global market. The money from this illicit trade funded the rearming of Saddam Hussein's military as well as filled the personal bank accounts of his top generals. Although the U.S. Navy was still operating in the region, they lacked the specialized law enforcement training and legal authority to board and capture vessels during peacetime. So they called in the Coast Guard.

Throughout the 1990s and early 2000s, Coast Guard boarding teams operating from Navy ships captured oil runners speeding toward the Iranian coast. These converted merchant ships would use barbed wire and steel plates welded to the hull to deter boarding parties, but the Coast Guard would use grappling hooks and disabling fire to sneak onboard. This prevented billions of dollars of oil from falling into the wrong hands, and put a huge dent in a criminal smuggling ring.

That's what the Coast Guard does, though. When we get the call – even on the darkest nights or in the stormiest seas – we swoop in with our grappling hooks and utility belts, to fight crime and save lives.

We're pretty much Batman.

#19 THE VIET CONG USED THE HO CHI MINH TRAIL BECAUSE THE COAST GUARD KEPT THEM OFF THE WATER

During the Vietnam War, insurgent fighters in the South smuggled in weapons from the North aboard fishing trawlers and junks. Since the Navy of the time only operated deep-draft warships, these smugglers could evade capture by simply sailing into shallow water where the Navy couldn't follow.

In response, a contingent of 17 Coast Guard patrol boats deployed to Vietnam. Retrofitted with mortars and extra machine guns, these 82' boats boarded over 230,000 suspected smuggling ships to search for weapons, and detained over 10,000 combatants. They provided fire support to U.S. forces on land, delivered troops up river for raids, and offered humanitarian assistance to locals. The operation was so successful that it forced the Viet Cong smugglers to abandon their shorter sea routes in favor of the more-arduous Ho Chi Minh Trail: a slog through the jungle that took weeks instead of days.

Eventually, the Navy acquired its own patrol boats, but even then the Coast Guard vessels proved superior in many ways: they carried more men and more firepower, could spend longer periods at sea, and – like all Coast Guard cutters – could withstand heavier weather.

Of course, all that meant was that the Navy took over patrolling during the fair-weather seasons, while the Coasties worked the monsoons.

#20 THE COAST GUARD HELPED CREATE THE NAVY SEALs

The Navy is a deep-water service, and has been for most of its existence. But in the Second World War (and let's face it, in every war), it turned out that most of the critical things were happening along the coast, not in the middle of the ocean. That meant the Navy lacked some of the capabilities necessary to scout the shoreline and gather valuable intelligence.

DO YOU SEE HITLER?
...NO.

The Office of Strategic Services (forerunner of the CIA) recognized this need. Europe had essentially turned into one giant fortress, and the only ways in were by air or water. So the OSS created the Maritime Unit: a special operations cell dedicated to developing, testing, and executing covert warfare missions at sea. Of the 226 men assigned to the unit, roughly a third were Coast Guard. The OSS specifically recruited them, citing their unique skills in small-boat handling, swimming, shallow-water sailing, and communications. Following their training, the members of the Maritime Unit deployed to Europe and Asia to carry out covert operations on behalf of the Allies.

The program was so successful that it was carried on after the war, and the tactics, methods, and tools developed by the Navy and Coast Guard for the Maritime Unit became the basis for the Navy SEALs, as well as all American combat swimmers.

In recognition of their contributions, in 1998, the Special Operations Command inducted the Unit's members as honorary members of the Special Forces. And, to make the circle complete, in 2010, two Coasties became the first non-Navy personnel to complete SEAL training and become full-fledged SEALs.

I'm not sure anyone else realizes why that's important.

OUR MISSION IS TO PILOT OUR SMALL BOAT ALONG THE COAST, BOARD THE PIRATE SHIP, RESCUE THE HOSTAGES, AND THEN GUARD THEM AS WE ALL SWIM TO THE EXTRACTION POINT. ANY QUESTIONS?
YEAH. HOW'S THE COASTIE SUPPOSED TO HELP?
NO IDEA.
"I mean, he didn't even bring sunglasses."

IMPORTANT EVENTS IN THE

1843: BUILT FOR SPEED, CLIPPER SHIPS BECOME THE PRIMARY MEANS OF TRADE WORLDWIDE. THEY CAN ROUND CAPE HORN OR REACH ASIA FASTER THAN OTHER SHIP, BUT LOSE FAVOR WHEN THE SUEZ CANAL OPENS IN 1869.

1865: CONFEDERATE COMMERCE RAIDER *SHENANDOAH* FIRES THE FINAL SHOT OF THE CIVIL WAR AT A WHALING FLEET IN THE ALEUTIAN ISLANDS - TWO MONTHS AFTER THE SOUTH ALREADY SURRENDERED.

1877: THE LIFE-SAVING SERVICE COMMISSIONS ARMY LIEUTENANT DAVID LYLE TO DESIGN A GUN THAT SHOOTS LINES OUT TO SINKING SHIPS. THE GUN STAYS IN USE UNTIL 1952, WHEN IT'S REPLACED BY ROCKET LAUNCHERS.

HISTORY OF COAST-GUARDING

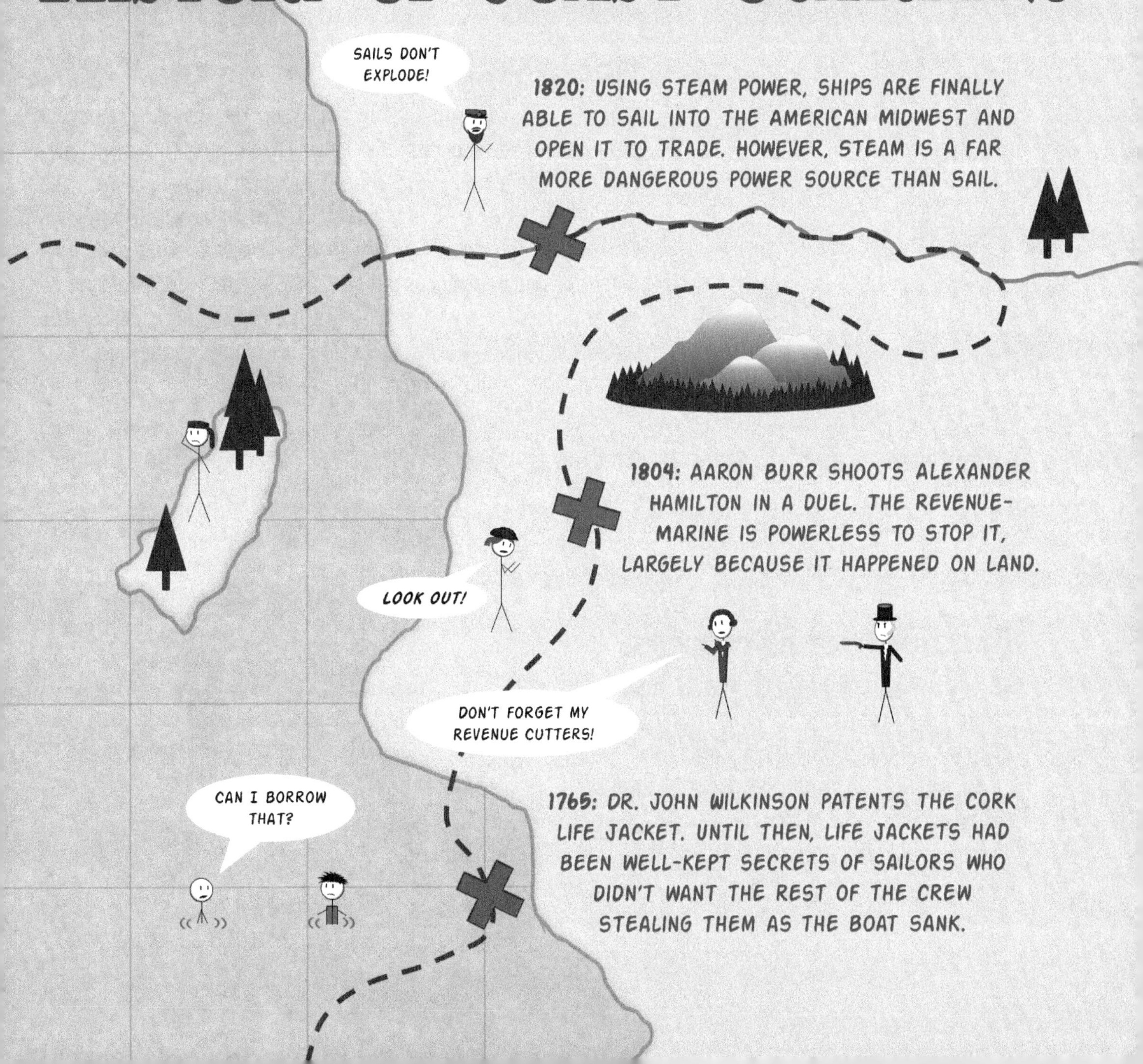
SAILS DON'T EXPLODE!
LOOK OUT!
DON'T FORGET MY REVENUE CUTTERS!
CAN I BORROW THAT?

1820: USING STEAM POWER, SHIPS ARE FINALLY ABLE TO SAIL INTO THE AMERICAN MIDWEST AND OPEN IT TO TRADE. HOWEVER, STEAM IS A FAR MORE DANGEROUS POWER SOURCE THAN SAIL.

1804: AARON BURR SHOOTS ALEXANDER HAMILTON IN A DUEL. THE REVENUE-MARINE IS POWERLESS TO STOP IT, LARGELY BECAUSE IT HAPPENED ON LAND.

1765: DR. JOHN WILKINSON PATENTS THE CORK LIFE JACKET. UNTIL THEN, LIFE JACKETS HAD BEEN WELL-KEPT SECRETS OF SAILORS WHO DIDN'T WANT THE REST OF THE CREW STEALING THEM AS THE BOAT SANK.

Shallow-Water Sailors

Norse Vikings

SAILING IN LONGSHIPS WITH DRAFTS OF AS LITTLE AS 3 FEET, VIKINGS MAY BE THE MOST SUCCESSFUL SHALLOW-WATER SAILORS EVER. THEY RAIDED ALL ALONG THE EUROPEAN COAST, STRIKING FEAR THROUGHOUT THE CONTINENT. MEANWHILE, NORSE EXPLORERS SAILED AS FAR WEST AS NEWFOUNDLAND AND - BY NAVIGATING THE RIVERS OF EUROPE - AS FAR SOUTH AS TURKEY. THEIR INFLUENCE ON MODERN MARINERS LIVES ON IN NAUTICAL TERMS, SHIP DESIGN, AND SAILING METHODS.

Renaissance Explorers

IF YOU WANT TO EXPLORE A NEW COASTLINE, YOU HAVE TO SAIL ALONG THE COAST. FOR THIS REASON, RENAISSANCE EXPLORERS RELIED ON THE CARAVEL: A SHALLOW-DRAFTED SHIP BUILT ON AN ARAB DESIGN. IT WAS THE CHOICE VESSEL OF EXPLORERS SUCH AS VASCO DE GAMA AND FERDINAND MAGELLAN, AND ITS SMALL DRAFT MADE IT PERFECT FOR SAILING AROUND OBSTACLES, UP RIVERS, OR INTO THE WATERS OF A NEW CONTINENT.

Throughout History

Caribbean Pirates

MOST PIRATES DIDN'T SAIL AROUND ON THE HIGH SEAS IN HUGE MAN-O'-WARS (AS COOL AS THAT MIGHT SOUND). RATHER, THEY FORMED FLEETS OF SMALL SHIPS AND WAITED NEAR CHOKE POINTS FOR FAT TREASURE GALLEONS TO SAIL THROUGH. ONCE THE GALLEONS WERE TRAPPED IN THE SHALLOWS AND COULDN'T MANEUVER, THE PIRATES WOULD OUTFLANK THEM AND SEIZE THEIR GOLD. THIS TACTIC IS STILL USED TODAY BY THE PIRATES OF SOMALIA AND SOUTHEAST ASIA. ...JUST WITH LESS GOLD.

The U.S. Coast Guard

THE MOST FEROCIOUS SHALLOW-WATER SAILORS OF ALL TIME, MODERN COASTIES STALK THE LITTORALS OF THE UNITED STATES IN GHOST-WHITE WARSHIPS. THEY OFTEN APPEAR AT THE SCENES OF SHIPWRECKS OR IN THE WAKE OF NATURAL DISASTERS. THEY ARE UNDETERRED BY WIND, SEAS, OR SOLID ICE, AND CAN GO DAYS OR WEEKS WITHOUT SLEEP. IF YOU SEE A COASTIE, THERE IS NO ESCAPE. THEY WILL FIND YOU, WHEREVER YOU ARE.

U. S. COAST GUARD

WATCH IT, NOOBS!
FIVE TIMES THE COAST GUARD WENT FIRST
U.S. COAST GUARD
73

#21 THE COAST GUARD HELPED THE WRIGHT BROTHERS FLY

If you know anything about the Wright Brothers' first flight in 1903, you probably remember that famous photograph: the one of Orville taking off while his brother runs alongside. But did you know that photograph – the only image of the first powered flight – was taken by a Coastie?

The Wrights' camp at Kitty Hawk was only a mile from Kill Devil Life-Saving Station. Three of the local surfmen grew curious about the Wrights' glider and found excuses to drop by: volunteering to carry lumber, haul equipment, or even bring the brothers their mail. They gradually befriended the inventors, and on the day of their historic flight, carried their glider a half mile to the launch track to set it up.

The surfmen's presence proved fortunate for aviation history – not just because they took a photo, but because they bore witness to the flight. While the Federal government initially dismissed the Wrights as crazy, it was hard for them to ignore the testimony of three brave surfmen.

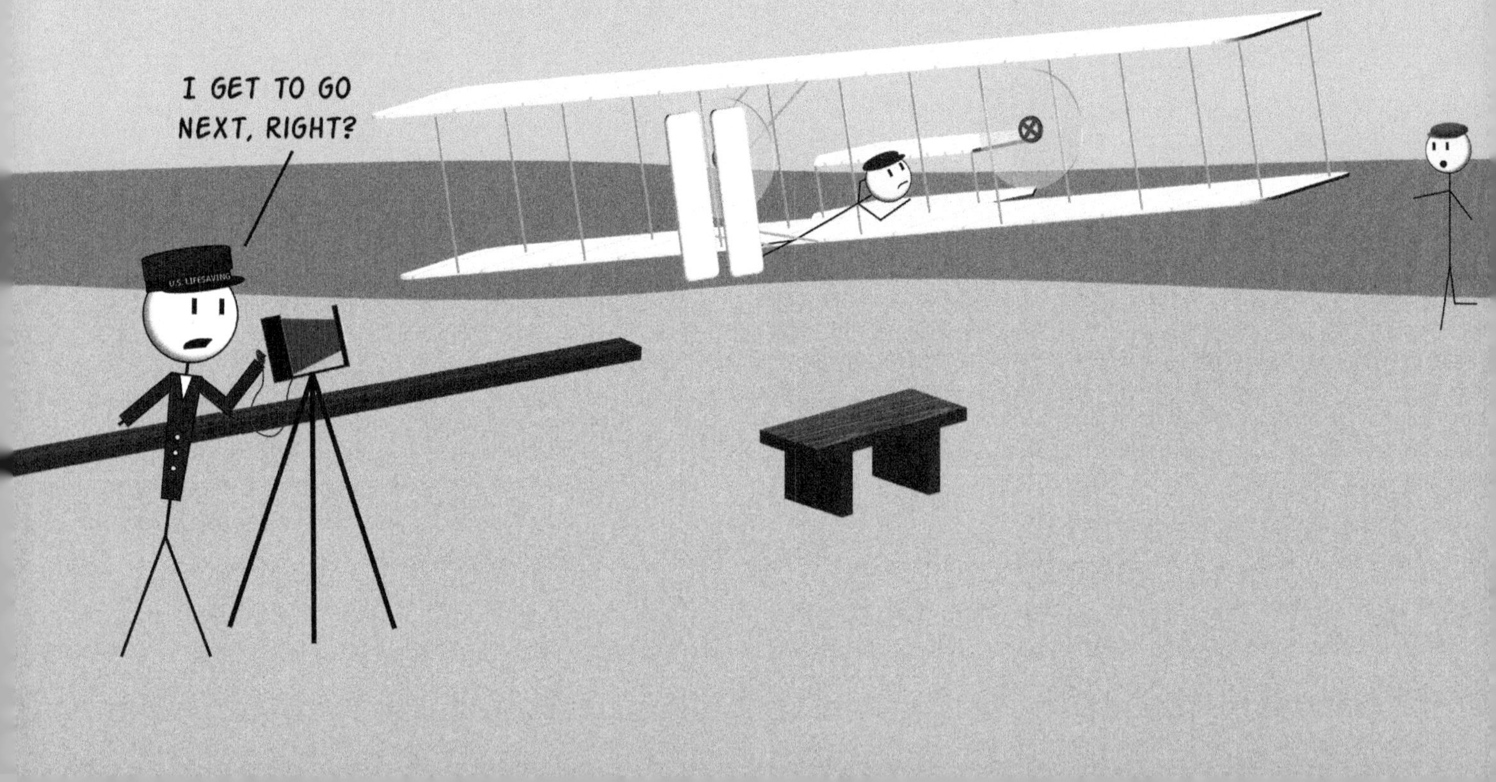
I GET TO GO NEXT, RIGHT?
U.S. LIFESAVING

#22 THE COAST GUARD HAD AN IRONCLAD

In 1861, engineer Edwin Stevens wanted to convince the Union Navy that his revolutionary ship design could help them beat the Confederates. 20 years earlier, he'd received a grant from Congress to build what was basically a floating gun battery, but his funding (and the Navy's interest) had run out before he could finish. This time, Stevens used his own money, fitting iron plates onto an existing ship. He installed heavy guns and a first-of-its-kind ballast system that let the vessel rise and sink in the water. However, the ship remained too experimental for Navy use, so Stevens offered her to the Revenue Cutter Service.

I'VE DESIGNED THIS SHIP SO SHE SINKS IN COMBAT.
WE'LL TAKE 10.

She became USRC *NAUGATUCK* in late 1861: the first ironclad in Union service, just a few months before the launch of the famous *MONITOR*. *NAUGATUCK* patrolled with the Navy the following spring, using her unique ballast system not only to partially submerge and avoid fire, but to test the depths of rivers and find channels for the rest of the fleet to use. She fought at the Battle of Hampton Roads – where the *MONITOR* dueled the Confederate ironclad *VIRGINIA* – and even exchanged fire with *VIRGINA*. True, *NAUGATUCK* may not have been as tough or as powerful as *MONITOR*, but like all Coast Guard cutters throughout our long history, she was slapped together from untested spare parts by a bunch of engineers who ran out of money. So she was definitely one of ours.

#23 THE COAST GUARD WAS FIRST TO PUT WOMEN IN CHARGE

Fighting the Axis in the Second World War required as much manpower as the United States could muster – alongside a resource that proved just as crucial: womanpower. Roughly 350,000 women served in uniform during the conflict, supplementing the millions of men drafted to fight. Of those 350,000 women, 12,000 joined the SPARs: the Coast Guard women's reserve.

The SPARs were initially recruited to perform clerical work, but immediately proved more capable. Many brought expertise from civilian careers as policewomen, photographers, farmers, or telephone operators. They trained at a number of locations all across the country, and even became the first women to train at a U.S. military academy when the Coast Guard Academy opened its doors to SPAR officers in 1943.

SPARs learned complex technical skills and held key positions of trust. Not only were they mechanics, electricians, and radar operators, they worked on top-secret government projects that helped determine the outcome of the war. In 1943, the Coast Guard sent Lieutenant Junior-Grade Vera Hamerschlag to take a course at MIT that was simply titled "Navigation." The following summer, she took charge of a small building in Chatham, Massachusetts with a 125-foot tall antenna outside. The building, known only as Unit 21, was a key component in the then-classified LORAN navigation system.

LORAN was critical to the war effort: it was a network of radio towers stationed all over the globe that allowed ships and aircraft to locate themselves within about a half-mile – an amazing feat at the time. This not only meant reduced fuel usage and safer travel, but deadlier bombing runs, more-precise naval patrols, and the ability to navigate even in bad weather. During the war, LORAN served 75,000 Allied units, but because of its top-secret nature, was known to almost no one.

When Hamerschlag took control of Unit 21, she was the only female. The plan was for her SPARs to slowly replace the male operators at the site once the women learned the job. It only took them a month.

Thankfully for Hamerschlag, the Coast Guard took a different tack toward its women's reserve than the other services. Military regulations at the time prohibited women from issuing orders to men, but the

Coast Guard circumvented this by stating that any female giving an order was doing so on behalf of her male superiors. This made the Coast Guard the first service to put women in charge of men (even if it was through a legal loophole) and allowed Hamerschlag to run her unit before the last man departed.

Because of the secrecy of their mission, Hamerschlag functioned more like the captain of a ship than the commander of a land unit. Her 10 SPARs lived and worked in a 50’ by 30’ building and maintained a 24-hour watch. They couldn’t tell anybody what they were up to – not even other SPARs – and couldn’t rely on anyone from the outside for repairs. Hamerschlag learned to fix plumbing, electronics, the coal furnace, and even the power generator on her own. She acted as personnel officer, operations planner, medical officer, and chief engineer. She even took her women to the gun range and taught them to shoot.

Unit 21 was one of the only all-female field units of the war, and may even have been the first operational unit commanded by a woman. Hamerschlag called it “as close to the front lines as it was possible for SPARs to be”: though thousands of miles away, their work helped bombers and ships hit their targets.

LITTLE TO THE RIGHT!

#24 A REVENUE CUTTERMAN WAS BASICALLY KING OF ALASKA

The Coast Guard has a lot of heroes, but there's only a handful I'd dare call true legends. One of those – without hesitation – is "Hell-Roaring" Mike Healy, de facto king of Alaska and bold captain of the *BEAR*.

File photo

Healy was born in 1839 in Macon, Georgia, the son of a slave and an Irish immigrant. To keep him and his siblings from being sold into slavery, his parents sent them to New York, where they all performed phenomenally: one brother became the first African-American bishop in North America. Another became the first African-American to receive a PhD, and later, President of Georgetown.

Michael, though, found academics boring. He took to sea on merchant ships and in 1865 joined the Revenue Cutter Service. Soon after, he was sent to Alaska, where he achieved his own first by becoming the first African-American to command a ship of the U.S. government. But that's not why he's a legend.

In 1886, Healy took charge of the *BEAR*: the greatest ship the RCS ever owned, captained at last by one of the finest seamen it ever employed. *BEAR* was a proto-icebreaker: a steam-powered sailing ship that could smash through icepack. In Healy's hands, *BEAR* became so well-known that Alaskans dubbed her "Healy's Fire Canoe," and some say she even helped inspire Jack London's novel *Sea-Wolf*.

In many of the places they sailed, Healy was the first and only representative of the U.S. government. He served at times as judge, doctor, ambassador, explorer, and king. He was better-known in the far-flung territory than any American President or ruler of Europe, and more respected than all of them combined. During his time in Alaska, he not only enforced laws and stopped poachers, but reintroduced reindeer from Siberia when local herds died off, mapped the mountains and rivers, sailed with naturalist John Muir on scientific expeditions, and built shelters on remote islands to shelter stranded sailors until rescue came.

Healy's job was tough: far from major ports, smugglers and ruffians flourished, and at times, he resorted to harsh tactics to enforce the law. On one occasion, he triced up a group of mutinous sailors by the wrists until they agreed to return to work, an act that got him court-martialed. His case wasn't helped by the fact that he drank heavily: a problem that his superiors had seen firsthand. In 1896, he was stripped of command, and his beloved *BEAR* sailed on without him.

Healy spent the next four years ashore as punishment. In 1900, though, at the peak of the gold rush, the RCS found itself short on captains. They gave Healy another ship, and he returned to Alaska to be king once more. He retired in 1903, and died a year later.

Like I said at the beginning, Healy is one of the true legends of the service. But he's also a man of many contradictions. On one hand, he was innovative, caregiving, and gregarious. On the other, he was harsh, reckless, and self-destructive. He enforced discipline on others, but couldn't enforce it on himself.

Maybe, though, I'm being too hard on Healy. His job was difficult, his responsibilities immense, and his options few. Perhaps the best way to understand him is just to let him speak for himself, in his own words:

WHEN I AM IN CHARGE OF A VESSEL, I ALWAYS COMMAND... I TAKE ALL THE RESPONSIBILITY, ALL THE RISKS, ALL THE HARDSHIPS THAT MY OFFICE WOULD CALL UPON ME TO TAKE.
I DO NOT STEER BY ANY MAN'S COMPASS BUT MY OWN.
GRRR!

Important Events In The

1886: The Statue of Liberty is the first electric lighthouse in the U.S. It's so dim that people quickly forget it was ever built as more than a giant statue.

I'M A LIGHTHOUSE?

1908: The increasing speed and safety of steamships makes sailing vessels obsolete. People abandon them at sea in droves, creating a hazard to everyone's new steamships.

CURSE YOU, IRONY!
CRASH

1931: Nine cyclones strike the coast of China. Together with high snowmelt, this causes massive floods that kill as many as 4 million people. It remains the worst natural disaster in recorded history.

History of Coast-Guarding

2010: The Coast Guard stops broadcasting LORAN signals worldwide. Although a few European transmitters remain, this marks the end of the once-global navigation system.

WHERE AM I?

1991: The Iraqi Army causes what may be the largest oil spill of all time by opening Kuwait's oil wells. So much oil seeps into sand and marshes around the Gulf that the true volume can't be counted.

1964: NYC-to-Europe ocean liner service peaks, with over 19,000 ship-borne passengers a week. A decade later, the industry is dead, replaced by jet travel.

YOUR MOVE, TSA

1945: Minefields make the North Sea unfishable during WWII, leading to a massive boom in fish stocks afterward. This aggressive approach to marine resource management is not tried again.

U.S. COAST GUARD

#25 THE COAST GUARD INVADED GREENLAND

Denmark surrendered to Germany in April of 1940, creating a huge conundrum for the U.S. (as well as robbing the Danes of peace and liberty, blah blah blah). See, Denmark, although a tiny European nation, actually owns Greenland. If the Nazis seized the island, it would not only give Germany a foothold on the west side of the Atlantic, it'd jeopardize one of the most critical and rare resources of the war: cryolite, a mineral critical to processing aluminum for aircraft. Greenland held the only mine available to the U.S.

The U.S. was still neutral in 1940, so the State Department frowned on sending in the Army or Navy to keep Germany out. They instead called on the Coast Guard, believing we'd be less threatening than the other services.

I'm not sure why they'd think that.

As an added bonus, the Coast Guard already had roughly a century's experience working in the Arctic. It summoned all of its ice-capable ships – including the *NORTHLAND* out of Alaska – and staged an almost-total takeover of Greenland. Under the authority of the Danish Ambassador in Washington – whom the U.S. continued to recognize as the legitimate Danish government – the Coast Guard sold weapons to the Greenlanders, which amounted to pulling the guns off of cutters and installing them on shore. Additionally, a few dozen Coasties were discharged from the service so they could 'volunteer' as guards for the cryolite mine. Since all of the maps and charts of Greenland were stuck in Copenhagen with the Germans, the Coast Guard also began the tedious work of remapping the entire frozen island from scratch.

IS THAT A ROCK OR AN ICEBERG?
IT'S A CUTTER.

"So…the least deadly of the three."

Over the next year, the Coast Guard escorted Army Engineers up from the U.S. to build proper defenses, as well as airfields, bases, and roads. The brilliant Coast Guard captain, Edward "Iceberg" Smith – who had spent years working in the Arctic and held a PhD in Oceanography from Harvard – took command of the Greenland Patrol, and of the *NORTHLAND*.

Then came the Germans.

Somewhere in the mountains along the coast, a German radio station buzzed out weather reports. While that may not seem like a big deal, it was awful if you were in the path of a German bomber: Hitler's Blitzkrieg strategy hinged on clear weather to run air raids and naval operations, and by stationing small teams of radiomen in Greenland, the Third Reich could predict storms for weeks in advance. A few weather reports from the far north could mean the difference between victory and defeat.

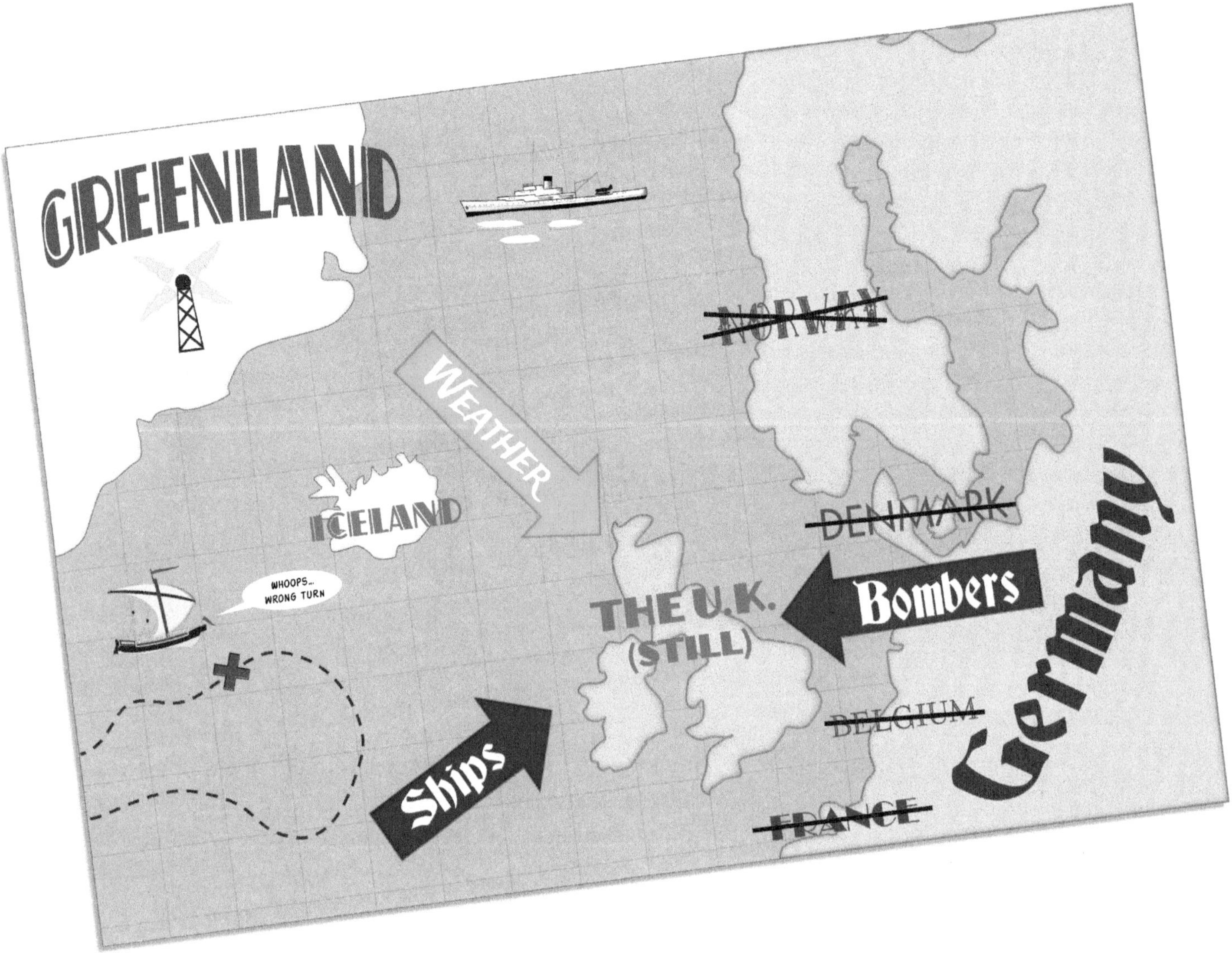

Three of Smiths' ships – one of which was actually the retrofitted *BEAR* – carried float planes. Smith dispatched the aircraft to scour the mountains and fjords for German outposts. He also organized a dogsled patrol, led by Danish hunters and native Greenlanders, to search for signs of German activity.

In September 1941, they had a break: *NORTHLAND* spotted a Norwegian fishing trawler tooling along the coast. Since Norway had been occupied by the Nazis for over a year, this raised Smith's suspicion. He sent a team to board the trawler, and among the passengers they found a man trying to hide radio gear. They questioned him, and found where the trawler had dropped off his compatriots.

That night, a party of 12 men from the *NORTHLAND* kicked in the door of a small hunting shack on the ice. The three German radio operators inside scrambled to burn their codebook, but the Coasties seized it first and took the men prisoner. This completed the first American combat action of World War II, three months before the U.S. was even in the fight and two months before the Coast Guard merged into the Navy. Of course, the fact that the U.S. was still neutral caused a bit of a problem: officially, the Germans weren't the enemy yet. The radiomen couldn't be held as prisoners of war when there wasn't technically a war for them to be prisoner in. So the Coast Guard arrested them for failing to go through customs.

See, firepower may work in wartime, but coast-power? That works anytime.

TO SUM UP...

The Coast Guard sails all over the world to carry out its many missions, and has done so since Washington was president. It has fought in every American war since 1790 and served on every continent.

Many people over the years have tried to make the case that we don't need a Coast Guard, but eventually, the needs of the nation (or a few strong storms) prove them wrong. Whether it's for our skill at search and rescue, our ability to fight through ice and waves, or our ability to adapt to any situation, we've always answered the (sometimes very strange) call.

It's true that we're the redheaded stepchild of the armed services, that we're underfunded and undermanned, but at the end of the day, our service is full of sharp, innovative people who always find a way to get the job done.

See, the Navy may have huge warships, the Air Force may have fighters and bombers, and the Marines and Army may have tanks and troops and artillery, but the Coast Guard will always manage to matter – always manage to tip the scales in some small way – because of the kinds of people it attracts and the ethos it inspires.

That must be it. Because it's certainly not our equipment.

Go Coast Guard.

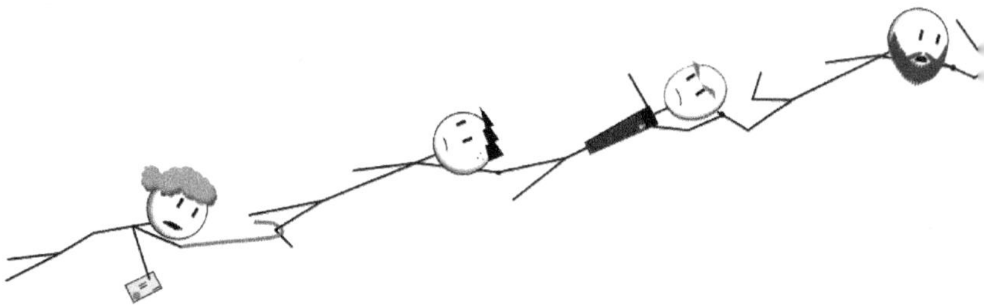

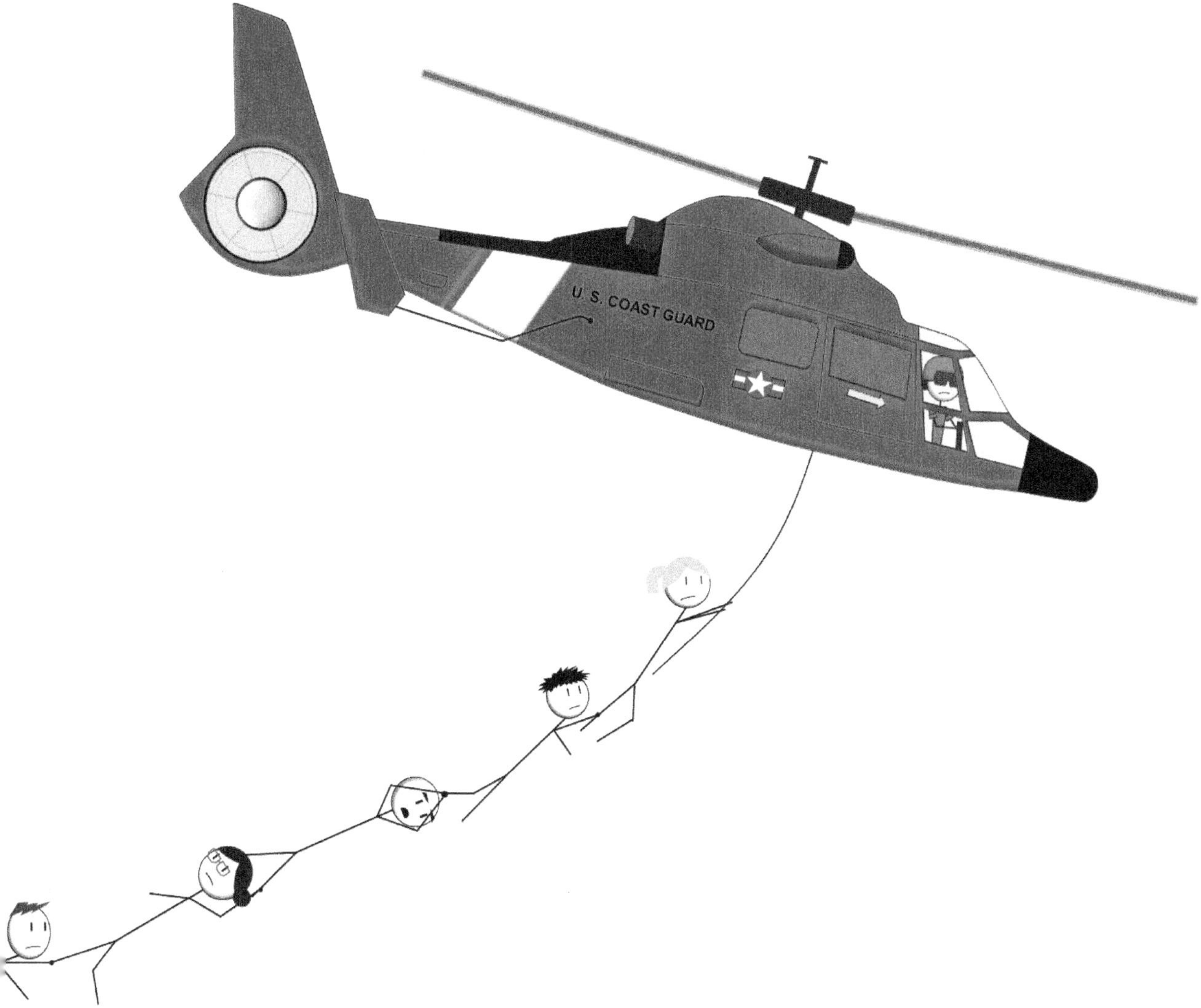
U. S. COAST GUARD

Sources

The following is a list of resources I consulted while creating this book, in case you'd like to do any additional reading and/or attempt to prove me wrong on something. I'd also encourage you to check out the materials available on the Coast Guard Historian's site at **uscg.mil/history**. Many of the documents I've cited here can be found on their page, along with additional information on almost all of the topics I've discussed. You can also reach out to me directly if you have questions.

1. Bennett, Michael E. "Guardian Spies: The Stories of Coast Guard Intelligence in World War II." American Intelligence Journal, vol. 27, no. 1. Fall 2009.

2. Bilby, Joseph G., and James M. Madden. *Hidden History of New Jersey at War*. Charleston, S.C.: History Press, 2011.

3. Braesch, Connie and Ryan White. "Coast Guard Heroes: William Trump." *Coast Guard Compass.* November 10, 2010. http://coastguard.dodlive.mil/2010/11/coast-guard-heroes-william-trump/

4. Braynard, Katie. "Honor, Respect, Devotion to Duty: LCDR Sean Plankey." *Coast Guard Compass.* July 11, 2014. http://coastguard.dodlive.mil/2014/07/honor-respect-devotion-to-duty-lcdr-sean-plankey/

5. Canney, Donald. "United States Revenue Marine Uniforms & Devices to 1908." Undated. http://www.uscg.mil/history/docs/usrcsuniforms1908.pdf

6. CBC News. "U.S. puts machine-guns on Great Lakes coast guard vessels." March 15, 2006. http://www.cbc.ca/news/canada/u-s-puts-machine-guns-on-great-lakes-coast-guard-vessels-1.622621

7. *Coast Guard On Foreign Shores*. Film, 25:40. United States Coast Guard. 1946. https://archive.org/details/CoastGuardOnForeignShores

8. Johnson, Robert Erwin. *Guardians of the Sea: History of the United States Coast Guard, 1915 to the Present*. Annapolis, Md.: Naval Institute Press, 1987.

9. King, Irving H. *George Washington's Coast Guard: Origins of the U.S. Revenue Cutter Service, 1789-1801*. Annapolis: Naval Institute Press, 1978.

10. Klug, Fritz. "Great Lakes have the most miles of coastline in contiguous US." MLive. April 2, 2013. http://www.mlive.com/news/index.ssf/2013/04/who_has_more_miles_of_coastlin.html

11. Lawless, Debra. *Chatham: From the Second World War to the Age of Aquarius*. Charleston, S.C.: History Press, 2010.

12. Lloyd, R. Jay. "Serving in Obscurity: United States Revenue Cutter Service Operations in the Gulf of Mexico During the Mexican American War 1846-1847." Thesis paper. New Mexico State University, May, 2007.

13. Lyne, Mary C. and Kay Arthur. *Three Years Behind the Mast: the Story of the Coast Guard SPARs*. Publisher unknown, 1946.

14. Modesto Radio Museum. "Voice of America Broadcasts From Coast Guard Cutter." http://www.modestoradiomuseum.org/voa%20courier.html

15. Oney, David. "Quentin R. Walsh." *Commandant's Bulletin*. June 1994, p. 26-27.

16. Thiesen, William H. "Guardians of the Gulf: A History of Coast Guard Combat Operations in Support of Operation Iraqi Freedom, 2002-2004." June 11, 2009. http://www.uscg.mil/history//articles/USCGinOIF.pdf

17. Thiesen, William H. "How the Coast Guard Earned Its Stripe." *Yachts International.* June 2012. http://www.yachtsinternational.com/lifestyle/lifestyle-special-features/how-the-coast-guard-earned-its-stripe/

18. Thompson, Robin J. "The Coast Guard and the Women's Reserve in World War II." United States Coast Guard. http://www.uscg.mil/history/articles/SPARS.pdf

19. Tilley, John A. *The Coast Guard and the Greenland Patrol.* Undated. http://www.uscg.mil/history/articles/GreenlandPatrol.pdf

20. Tulich, Eugene N. "The Coast Guard in South East Asia During the Vietnam Conflict." Undated. http://www.uscg.mil/history/articles/h_tulichvietnam.asp

21. U.S. State Department. "Rush-Bagot Pact, 1817 and Convention of 1818." https://history.state.gov/milestones/1801-1829/rush-bagot

22. Ulm, Aaron Hardy. "Our 'Little White Navy' – Must It Go?" *The Dearborn Independent.* January 8th, 1921. Library of Congress: Chronicling America Archive.

23. United States Coast Guard Historian's Office, compiled. "Project Sea Hunt Study." 17 November, 2014. http://www.uscg.mil/history/ops/sar/ProjectSeaHunt/ProjectSeaHuntStudy.pdf

24. United States Coast Guard. "Ask an astronaut." *YouTube* video, 6:52. July 24, 2012. https://www.youtube.com/watch?v=USbgaYWKnwI

25. United States Coast Guard. "Boeing PB-1G 'Flying Fortress.'" Washington, D.C.: U.S. Coast Guard Historian. http://www.uscg.mil/history/aviation/Boeing/Boeing_PB1.pdf

26. United States Coast Guard. "Some Unusual Incidents in Coast Guard History." U.S. Coast Guard Public Information Division, 1950. http://www.uscg.mil/history/articles/USCG/1950_SomeUnusualIncidents.pdf

27. Weydert, David. "The Coast Guard's Ironclad." *Coast Guard Mid Atlantic.* April 3, 2015. http://coastguard.dodlive.mil/2014/07/honor-respect-devotion-to-duty-lcdr-sean-plankey/

28. Wiarda, Jonathan S. "The U.S. Coast Guard in Vietnam: Achieving Success in a Difficult War." *Naval War College Review*, vol. LI, no. 2. Spring 1998.

About the Author

Brian Runion is the creator of the blog and webcomic *The Claw of Knowledge*, a thing he made while trying to do something else. You can find him online at clawofknowledge.com, on Facebook, or by screaming 'The Claw of Knowledge' loudly at your mobile device.

Brian grew up in the Pacific Northwest, where trees and mountains are appropriately-sized. He graduated from the U.S. Coast Guard Academy 2-3 years before you got there, back when it was still tough. He received his Masters in Fancy Political Stuff from the University of Michigan, and now uses those advanced skills to make cartoons in PowerPoint. He hates coffee, water chestnuts, and writing 'About the Author' pages. He likes seaweed snacks, Zipfizz, and rain.

CPSIA information can be obtained
at www.ICGtesting.com
Printed in the USA
BVOW07*2110120916
461899BV00002B/4/P

9 780692 564899